BRITAIN IN OLD PHOTOGRAPHS

AROUND CLITHEROE

CATHERINE ROTHWELL

ALAN SUTTON PUBLISHING LIMITED

Alan Sutton Publishing Limited
Phoenix Mill · Far Thrupp · Stroud
Gloucestershire · GL5 2BU

First Published 1995

Copyright © Catherine Rothwell

Cover photographs: front: Castle Street,
Clitheroe; back: the post office, Wray.

British Library Cataloguing in Publication Data.
A catalogue record for this book is available from
the British Library.

ISBN 0-7509-0971-4

Typeset in 9/10 Sabon.
Typesetting and origination by
Alan Sutton Publishing Limited.
Printed in Great Britain by
Ebenezer Baylis, Worcester.

Dedicated to my grandmother, Catherine Hoghton.

Contents

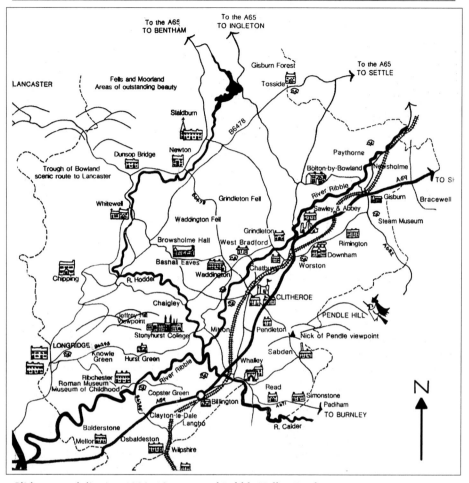

Clitheroe and district, 1993. (Courtesy of *Ribble Valley Explorer*)

Introduction

Roman cavalry splashing through the ford at Hell Hole on their regular rides between Ribchester fort and Elslack some 1,800 years ago must have been impressed. The Devil himself was believed to live at Hell Hole when the river was in flood. In direct contrast, the vale through which the rivers Ribble, Calder and Hodder wind with Pendle Hill in the background, a glorious mass of trees following the bright course of waters, became known as Paradise. By the nineteenth century 'Looking Towards Paradise' was a favourite picture postcard.

By 1900, in somewhat oblique contrast, Clitheroe was dubbed 'Tramps' Paradise' when 5,000 of them, including Gentleman Tom, were passing through, drawn less by scenery than by Mr Martin's supper of 6 oz of bread and a pint of porridge. All summer Tom travelled between the workhouses of Blackpool, Kirkham and Clitheroe (where help was liberal). The more wealthy who could afford to ride enjoyed the luxuries of the last remaining coaching inns of the area – the Swan and Royal, the Ribblesdale Arms and the Swan at Clitheroe, Gisburn and Whalley respectively.

For centuries the fear of witchcraft remained strong in this region. Houses and cottages had a witch post on top of which was placed a crooked sixpence to speed butter churning and to counteract spells. The farmer might place a crown piece in the churn or make a sudden thrust into the cream with a red-hot poker that hissed and despatched any budding Demdike or Chattox. In the ceremony of 'lating the witches' on Longridge Fell on 1 November candles were carried, which everyone hoped would burn steadily between eleven and midnight so that evil would be overcome for the forthcoming season. The road through the Trough was the last ever trudged by the Lancashire Witches. From the farms and villages of the Pendle area ten were sent to the scaffold, nine at Lancaster and one at York. The names of Alice Nutter, Chattox and Demdike are so well remembered that at Hallowe'en some people still make a midnight pilgrimage to Pendle Hill.

Other Pendle customs include 'beating the bounds' when the elders 'beat' the youngsters with canes as they perambulated the parishes. This was to impress the boundaries upon their minds. At mid-Lent braggat or spiced ale was drunk with Simnel cake; on Easter Day flat, spiced cakes were carried and eaten. In early spring dock pudding featured in Ribble and Calder Valley eating contests, where as many as fifty people would compete.

> When Pendle wears a woolly cap,
> The farmers all may take a nap

was one of many rhymes about the weather, but the farmers were never caught napping at the ploughing matches, which were keenly contested.

'Grand Old Pendle' was one of a chain of beacons which were fired at momentous times. A heap of stones there may indicate the site of Malkin Tower, home of Demdike, the self-confessed witch. When George Fox, founder of the Quaker movement, made the ascent in 1652 he was greatly impressed by the atmosphere and the view. On the night before battle Oliver Cromwell chose to sleep on a well-guarded table at Stonyhurst, not far from the 'Paradise' already mentioned.

Horse races, the first of which was held 380 years ago, attracted people from all around. At Horrocksford pastures in 1823 prizes included two handsome silver cups, a purse of gold and an excellent saddle. Bare-back riding on lime kiln ponies must have been exciting, surpassed only by the action of a notorious Preston character 'Touch' Duckworth, who brought his black bear. Out of sheer spleen because his horse, Sheep Stealer, did not win he unmuzzled the beast and let it run amidst the spectators.

Of the ancient forests once hunted by Norman dukes Bowland is one of the last remaining wildernesses. In the 1930s E. King of Pimlico Road advised that, for a reasonable charge, 'the best way to explore the beauties of the Trough of Bowland is to go by car . . . ride in comfort and perfect ease in our luxurious Rolls-Royce cars'.

More important and relevant to our own time, however, is what still remains. At Edisford Bridge on 1 June 1985 Mike Harding, President of the Ramblers' Association, with Sir Derek Barber ceremonially opened the Ribble Way, linking Longton with Gisburn and making accessible a dramatic range of scenery. Along this wonderful route are towns, villages, churches and halls, all rich in history. A walk upstream from Sawley Abbey through Cold Park Wood and Sheep Wood takes you through a deep gorge before reaching Gisburn. Downstream brings you to Clitheroe with its Norman keep, the second smallest in the country, which celebrated its 800th anniversary in 1986.

Among Clitheroe Corporation's plate is a long, silver mace presented in 1672. On the day of the Mayor's election this is on show with a massive silver punch bowl. Traditionally, the Town Sergeant, in robes and cocked hat, carries the mace, followed by the Head Waiter bearing the steaming punch bowl containing a brew made from a secret ancient recipe. 'Prosperation to the Corporation' is the great shout that goes up, a shout that has reverberated through the years from the town's first Charter, whose green wax seal shows Henry de Lacy on horseback, visor down, carrying a shield and holding a drawn sword.

Around Clitheroe in Old Photographs attempts not only to evoke the atmosphere of day-to-day events experienced by our ancestors in an old market town, but also underlines a present heritage. These old photographs remind us of what we dare not lose. It is interesting to note that the Ribble Valley has officially been set as 'the centre of the kingdom' since the Ordnance Survey named a spot near Dunsop Bridge as the heart of Great Britain.

On a personal note, during my quest, fragments of verse from over a hundred years ago, written as a girl by my grandmother, who was born at Low Moor, have so frequently come to mind, I felt keenly that I was treading in her footsteps.

Section One

CLITHEROE

The corner of Moor Lane and Castle Street, 1900.

Clitheroe Castle keep, late 1960s. Ilbert de Lacy, a Norman knight who fought at the Battle of Hastings, became one of the most powerful men in the north of England when he was rewarded with a huge tract of land stretching from Clitheroe to Pontefract. He could ride from the castle at Clitheroe to his castle at Pontefract 50 miles away, resting in halls which he also owned. Henry de Lacy, Lord of the Honour of Clitheroe 1147–77, granted the borough's first Charter and a town was formed. The streets of Clitheroe were named Castlegate, Marketgate and Wellgate. Blackburnshire, Ribchester, Chipping and the Forest of Bowland became the 'Honour of Clitheroe' and administration moved from Blackburn to Clitheroe Castle where courts were held.

Clitheroe Castle set on its limestone knoll, drawn by G. Pickering in 1832. Longridge Fell can be seen in the background and the parish church, St Mary Magdalene, on another limestone mound on the right. This and the castle chapel of St Michael date from the eleventh century. The last siege in the long history of the castle took place at the time of the Civil War, when 4,000 troops, disenchanted with their leader, Colonel Ashton, and the fact that they had not been paid, marched from Bowland and entered the castle. They were soon routed and the castle ordered to be slighted so that it no longer presented a threat to the Commonwealth. St Michael's, within the castle walls and considered to be the parish church of the forests, was razed when the castle was dismantled. The castle with its 6 acres of surrounding land was considered a township in itself, exempt from the jurisdiction of the borough of Clitheroe, a right which continued until 1895. 'Orme the Englishman' was the last Lord of the Manor at Clitheroe.

Cromwell's Bridge over the River Hodder, 1961. Known as the 'Brig of Hoder' in 1648 when 8,000 of Cromwell's soldiers marched across, this is a pack-horse bridge. Its graceful, fragile structure can be fully appreciated from the Lower Hodder Bridge, which stands alongside.

The Castle House, *c.* 1890. Built in 1723 as a residence for the Steward, who lived here with his family and servants, the house included kitchen, buttery, cellar, milk house, hall and parlour. It now houses Clitheroe Museum and the North West Sound Archives.

Edmund Parker, shown here in an eighteenth-century engraving, was a Bowbearer of Bowland Forest. Along with the Stewards, the Bowbearers were the principal officers of the forests or chases, land over which the lord could hunt. Tenants were heavily fined at the Steward's Court for cutting down trees or slaying deer. The keeping of any dog not small enough to pass through the 'stirrup' or 'doggange' (dog gauge) was unlawful. Large dogs could threaten the lord's game, yet one of his ancient rights was to claim 'putura', which was the taking of meat, free, for his own hunting dogs, from people who lived in the forest. See also p. 45.

Roger Kenyon, in a portrait painted in the 1690s. Roger Kenyon was MP for Clitheroe and Governor of the Isle of Man. Related to the Rigby family, he was also Clerk of the Peace from 1663 to 1698. This was a hereditary post in the fifteenth and sixteenth centuries, and the Rigbys and Kenyons feature in an uninterrupted sequence as holders of this important sinecure for two hundred years. (Courtesy of Lancashire Record Office)

Henthorn Farm, *c.* 1870. Antecedents of Clitheroe lady Mrs Laura Clark farmed here, using time-honoured methods. Gangs of men were employed to mow the meadows with long-bladed scythes. They were followed by the tedders, who used hay forks to turn and stook the corn into 'cock-ups'. These would be left to dry and ripen in the sun. Mechanical mowers and 'tedding machines' replaced these methods in the late nineteenth century. John Winkley of King Street, Clitheroe, supplied farm carts and implements. He was a sawyer and hay-rake maker. Theo Wilson of King Street was a dealer in bar and hoop iron mowing and hay-making machines.

Fishes and Pegs Hill Farm, Henthorn, between Edisford and Mitton, *c.* 1890. The farm's land sloped down to the river where fishes were caught, using pegs as floats, which is how the farm got its name. Of 580 families in Clitheroe, 76 were employed in agriculture.

Mytton Flatts, Clitheroe, 1880s. At Flatts Row lived John Hodgson, a farrier who sold neatsfoot oil and 'Gallipoli' for dressing leather harness. In the 1840s John Haworth, manager at Primrose Mill, lived at Flatts Row. (In older documents the name is given as Mytton, although the modern spelling is Mitton.)

Stainforth pack-horse bridge over the River Ribble, *c.* 1927. Built by Samuel Watson in the seventeenth century, Stainforth is another example of a fine bridge, with its narrow, low parapet designed to ease the passage of ponies with their loads of limestone, coal and other goods between Lancaster and York.

Timothy Feather, hand-loom weaver, 1903. Hand-loom weaving was supplanted by machinery in the 1840s and Mr Feather was one of the last exponents of the craft still working by hand in the area. His work was prized and he was still taking orders from people who were prepared to wait to obtain their goods.

Bailey Brothers, corn millers, Market Place, c. 1890. The Baileys' premises were over a wholesale grocer's shop, and a drinking fountain stood opposite. In 1905 both the fountain and the corn millers' premises were demolished, the latter replaced by the Carnegie Library, which opened that same year. Beyond Market Place this view looks towards York Street, which was built in 1826 as part of a new road to Chatburn. In York Street there is still a heavy, studded door that once flanked the entrance to the town gaol, which was used until the 1880s. In 1834 the Royal Grammar School building was moved stone by stone to York Street from its situation in the churchyard where it had been since 1782.

Church Street, with the ghostly keep of the castle in the background, *c.* 1880. Morgan Dewhurst, boot and shoemaker, may have had his shop on the right where the two men are standing. Church Street leads into Market Place and Castle Street, where James Wilson, auctioneer and town crier, lived; until 1826 it was the main route from Clitheroe to Skipton. There was a church here in 1122, long before a road system evolved. The present church of St Mary Magdalene was built in 1828. About twelve years later the spire became twisted but this fault was rectified in 1969. Inside is a memorial plate to Dr John Webster, Vicar of Mytton, also headmaster of the Grammar School. He lived during the Civil War and in a long treatise published in 1677 he denounced witchcraft.

A poster from Queen Victoria's reign, dated 2 July 1852, issued by the Borough of Clitheroe to let all eligible voters know that Thomas Garnett, Mayor of the Borough, intended to be present at the hustings in Market Place at 10 a.m. on 6 July 1852 to proclaim himself a candidate for parliamentary election. Feelings ran high in the town. James Heaton of Clitheroe, a newspaper reporter, produced political 'squibs' for electioneering purposes which so inflamed some voters that it led to blows and rowdiness, which frightened the peaceful townsfolk (see p. 18).

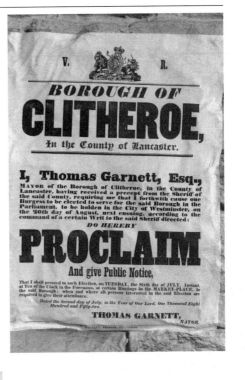

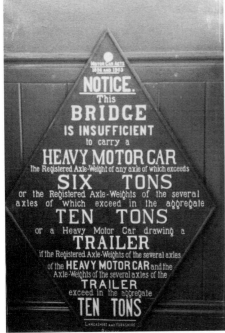

A Lancashire and Yorkshire Railway heavy iron notice at Clitheroe station, 1904. It warns that under the Motor Car Acts of 1896 and 1903 the bridge will not carry a heavy motor car or weight of more than 10 tons. This notice is now one of many artefacts owned and exhibited by the Clitheroe Railway Society who have worked very hard to reinstate a rail service between Clitheroe and Blackburn.

Moor Lane Chapel, 1890s. Revd Benjamin J.H. Shaw was minister. He lived at Holmes Cottage, Woone Lane. The board on this 1797 building reads 'United Free Churches'.

The scene at the political hustings in Clitheroe, photographed by E. Buck, 1868. This was the last year in which hustings were erected. In 1878 the Riot Act was read from the steps of Mr Lofthouse's Swan and Royal in Castle Street and a detachment of Lancers charged the crowd. Blows were often exchanged at parliamentary elections.

Passengers on Hacking ferry, 1935. Henry Fielding and Annie Longden are at the front, behind the ferryman. Mrs Warren, Sam Gallagher, Maud Tower and Burt Fielding are also on board. Ferries crossed the River Ribble at Hacking Hall, Dinckley and, before the bridge was built, at Grindleton where the boat was supplied by the Tucker family.

Good Friday celebrations, Brungerley, 1906. Thousands flocked into Clitheroe from Burnley and Padiham, some walking over Nick o' Pendle, others coming by wagonette. The railway brought people from Blackburn and Darwen. An 1880 pictorial handbook to the valley of the Ribble refers to Eli Tucker of Brungerley Farm and his sons, David and Charles, who supplied the boats for this event.

Left to right: Clarence Standen, Mahlon Chilion Robinson, Bert Wilkinson and Charles Gorton, 1928. Mr Robinson, who died in 1952, was owner of a wheelwright's and joiner's shop in Queen Street, Whalley. It was this team that built the Hacking ferry boat.

Dr A.W. Musson and his son, Francis, 1898. Dr Musson lived at 11 King Street and owned the first motor car within a 25 mile radius of Clitheroe. The Benz car is seen in the drive of Waddow Hall. At that time Dr Musson was one of six surgeons in and around Clitheroe.

Brungerley Bridge, 1900. The Tucker family provided swings, a roundabout and a tea-room. Steps built down into the river and changing huts nearby made bathing possible.

A 'twister' at work, c. 1910. The twister's job involved hand-twisting new warp into a harness loom in the Pendle cotton industry. He performed about a hundred twistings in an hour, after joining together two threads to form a temporary knot.

Three bobbin winders at the Low Moor factory, *c.* 1906. Most of the workers lived in Low Moor village where John Parker, the first owner of the factory, began to build cottages for mill hands in 1851. Soon there were 248 dwellings and a population of 1,272. The girls' hair was dressed high and enclosed in white caps to prevent it from getting caught in the flying bobbins and whirling belts on the machinery. At the centenary of Low Moor Mills, celebrated on 14 April 1899, 1,197 persons attended dinner, for which 800 lb of beef and 700 lb of fish were ordered. Medals were struck bearing the inscription '1799–1899 William Garnett, Head of the firm Thomas Garnett and Sons'. The Albion Bobbin Works in Clitheroe, a three-storey building with a saw mill and a shuttle shop, was purpose built. Next to the mill was Albion House, behind Clitheroe railway station. In the nineteenth century workers in the cotton mills toiled for sixty hours a week and were paid according to how much they produced. The growth of Clitheroe town was due mainly to the cotton industry.

Castle Street, Clitheroe, *c.* 1907. The New Café, H. Myers, Boots and Cunningham's Garage can be seen, with the Swan and Royal Hotel Garage and Bait Stables in the distance. Of the towns situated on the River Ribble Clitheroe was second in importance to Preston. On market days goods were laid out in the triangular area in Market Place and the stalls extended along Castle Street. By the end of the nineteenth century a self-contained site had to be provided. Market charges were 2*d* for a cow and 4*d* for a horse, when sold. Since the days of the Normans a market has been held in Clitheroe every Saturday and during one period five fairs a year were held, which were considered great occasions. Clitheroe possesses thirteen ancient Charters relating to privileges granted to the free burgesses of the town over a period of seven centuries.

The Swan and Royal Hotel at the top of Castle Street, *c.* 1926. In the centre is the Carnegie Library, opened with a golden key by John Eastham in 1905. The library clock was set going on the same day by Mayoress Mrs J.T. Whipp. Bicycles were obviously in vogue. 'Why hike it when you can bike it?' advertised Benthams of 14 Market Place. Castle Street, King Street and Moor Lane had become busy shopping centres, expanding on the crafts which had existed since the town's beginning. In the 1920s extra cables were laid to bring electricity. The town's water was originally supplied by three wells; Town's Well, Wellgate; Stock's Well, Parsons Lane; and one in Well Terrace. Jemmy Driver also hawked water around the streets, supplying two tins for a halfpenny. In 1854 the Clitheroe Waterworks Company was formed, the first sod of Marylebone Reservoir being cut in spring 1855 by John Eastman. This reservoir had a capacity of 500,000 gallons and by the next year 471 houses in the borough were receiving water from a 9 in diameter pipe. The 1878 Corporation Act empowered the taking over the waterworks and gasworks companies and a second main was laid. Alderman J. Garnett cut the first sod of the second reservoir on 23 April 1887. Known as Lowcock's, its capacity was twenty-five times greater than the original reservoir, which is now used only as reserve storage. In 1957 a new 15 in main was laid from the reservoir through the town and further supplies became available from two bore holes. Fylde Water Board took over in 1963.

The ox roast of 1902, held to celebrate the coronation of Edward VII. The men in white coats in the centre are the ox roasters. Clitheroe had a tradition of ox roasts and other Lancashire towns, notably Fleetwood, called on their expertise.

Standen Hall, near Clitheroe, 1902. This was once the home of Arthur Viscount Southwell and a French aristocrat, Sophia Maria Joseph. They lived in France until the Revolution of 1792 when they escaped with other members of the family. By 1833 Colonel Aspinall, who laid the foundation stone of the Sunday school, lived here.

A glimpse of Castle Street showing Briggs' entry (right), early 1900s. The Café and Commercial Hotel catered for travellers and visitors. The New Café below was a popular baker's and pastry cook's premises. 'Storage Stables' indicated that horse traffic was still very much a way of life.

Whalley Road, early 1900s. With no traffic to watch out for, all eyes are on that novelty, the street photographer, except for one small boy. Boys, ladies and delivery cart man are trying to stand very still as directed.

Queen Mary's School, 1912. This was the old Royal Grammar School, which had been founded in 1554 under a Charter granted by Mary Tudor. It was free to everyone. The girls later had their own grammar school in Chatburn Road, but in 1985 Clitheroe Royal Grammar School became co-educational and by 1991 was grant maintained.

Little Moor, 1890. Before the 1788 Enclosure Act Little Moor was a long tract of moorland, with which several ancient names were associated, including Goose Butts and Upper and Lower Holme. Today's reminders are Holmes Mill and Holmes Cottage. The first houses were built in 1810 by John Bateson, landlord of the Swan Inn.

Mrs Kay, 'Grandmother Campey's mother'. Born *c*. 1843, Mrs Kay made treacle dabs for sale on Clitheroe, Burnley and later Blackburn markets where she also introduced 'butter toffee'.
Photographs were known as 'likenesses' a hundred years ago when the Leeds photographer William Smith invited Mrs Kay into his studio, wearing her best bonnet and gown. In those early days Mr Smith could produce 'enlargements up to life size' if so desired.

Luke Taylor and Mrs Taylor (Alice Wilkinson before marriage) *c*. 1880. Luke, a cotton spinner, was born in 1849 and died from food poisoning on 8 September 1921, aged 72. They lived at 24 West View, Clitheroe, and had fourteen children. One of them, Rifleman Thomas Taylor, was killed in the trenches in the First World War, which later also claimed Luke, another son.

The Coronation Ox of 1911. Ten hundredweight of wood and ten of coal were used, the roast being turned and basted throughout the night. After twelve hours it was ready. A macabre photograph exists of the ox before slaughter, surrounded by the Coronation Committee.

The Harrison family of Henthorn outside their home, *c.* 1870. Among them is Mary (probably the older lady seated on the right), who died on 9 April 1882 aged 79 and whose maiden name was Wilkinson. She came from Waddington and was born and raised in one of the old leper cottages at Edisford.

The Chief Constable of Clitheroe, c. 1900. Since 1839 Clitheroe, the second oldest borough in Lancashire (Wigan was the first), has enjoyed the privilege of being able to organize its own police force headed by a Chief Constable. In 1947 the town amalgamated with the Lancashire County when control of the police force and education passed to the County. (Courtesy of Clitheroe Museum)

Sam Green, c. 1870. Sam Green was the Clitheroe Grammar School music teacher of tonic sol-fa, a system of musical notation and sight singing which was developed in 1850 by Revd John Curwen, a Congregationalist minister. It was taught throughout schools in the nineteenth century and into the twentieth. The Church of England National School in Clitheroe, under head teacher Mr Langshaw, also instructed the children in tonic sol-fa. (Courtesy of Clitheroe Museum)

Clitheroe railway station, 1875. One of Jenkins's 0–6–0 engines has shunted the yard clear of coal. This engine was fitted with a large headlamp which had different coloured lenses to indicate codes. Two headlamps could be mounted side by side. The first sod of the local line was cut by Lord Ribblesdale on 30 December 1846 when a silver spade and a mahogany wheelbarrow were used. Some Clitheroe people, from fear and distrust, refused to use the railway. At the age of 70, Peter Nowell of the Boar's Head trudged all the way to a funeral at Whalley while his family went by train. Miss Ellen Haworth, postmistress of Pendleton, never went on a train; her father forbade it. In 1850 Joseph Marland became the first engine driver on Clitheroe railway.

A group of workmen from the Portland Cement Company, 1918. Cement production in Clitheroe began in the early 1900s, when Messrs Spackman owned a limestone quarry. The company later became known as Ribblesdale Cement, and is now the giant Castle Cement, whose chimney dominates the town. The plant was introduced in 1935 and building has continued. Long ago limestone was carried by Galloway ponies known as Lime Gals, a hardy breed fitted with panniers to carry loads to the coast and industrial areas. The pony train returned with fish, oysters and other items needed in Clitheroe. Slater's Directory of 1885 lists the Bold Venture Lime Company, Chatburn; Richard Briggs and Sons, Salthill, Clitheroe; William Veevers and Company and Horrocksford Lime Works.

West Bradford Falls, *c.* 1918. The salmon ladder shown enabled fish to travel upstream at spawning time. At this ancient village close to Clitheroe a corn mill, powered by a water wheel, was converted to a cotton mill in 1867. In 1960 the mill was bought by the firm Trutex but is now to be swept away.

Gisburn Mill, July 1905. This view is from a postcard to Clitheroe, which bears the message: 'This weather will suit the hay.' The mill had a dam, water wheel and goit and was used as a saw mill in 1911. The farmer who sent the message may also have had an interest in Gisburn hiring fair, held around 28 June when rough drovers brought cattle down the High Street for sale and itinerant Irish labourers presented themselves for hire to help with the haymaking on the farms around Clitheroe. Along the main street were stalls selling farm implements. Morris dancers and brass bands attended the Field Days. The scene is not far from the impressive gorge now waymarked along the Ribble Way.

Clitheroe from the castle keep, 1904. The proliferation of mills is evident; at one time there were seventeen. On the left is the Starkies Arms and the parish church of St Mary Magdalene, whose spire was added in 1845.

A typical fine weather scene at Brungerley Bridge, July 1922. When the river froze it was thronged with skaters, among them Clement Hoghton (see p. 95), known as 'the champion one-legged skater'. His mother was Catherine, née Garnett, of Low Moor.

Six weavers in the bobbin shop, with the 'tackler' in the background wearing a typical flat, cloth cap, 1911. The weaver sitting in the middle is holding a shuttle in both hands. The decorations were in honour of King George V's and Queen Mary's coronation. When children were allowed to work in the cotton mills a Manchester master advertised for '... children from 8–11 years. Parents offered £3 for the first year, £4 for the second year, £5 for the third year'. A Clitheroe worker reported: 'I was a bobbin winder when I was eight and when nine my father taught me to weave on the loom we had in the kitchen. The term "cotton" was then also applied to woollen material. From flax, fustians were made. We worked on the night shift for 4–5 long years, from 7 in the evening to 6 in the morning.' One mill owner 'agreed with the parish to take one idiot child with every twenty normal'.

St James's Football Team, winners of the Clitheroe Sunday School League Division Two Championship 1920–1, with the cup and medals presented to them. St James's Cricket Club commenced playing on Little Moor in about 1900.

Ellen Harrison seated outside Henthorn Farm near Mytton, *c.* 1880. Richard Harrison, along with others, collected money to provide the clock in Mytton church tower. It ushered in the New Year, striking for the first time on 31 December 1897.

The nine founder members of Clitheroe Golf Club, *c.* 1900. The first bicycle club was formed in 1884, while football games up and down the town, starting from Alleys Green, began even earlier. (Courtesy of Clitheroe Museum)

Clitheroe District Golf Club, 13 August 1921. Back row, left to right: H. Boothman, W. Lupton, B.E. Jones, H. Cook, T. Clough, A. Denham. Second row: G. Garstang, G. Wilkinson, F.D. Hay, D. Lister, H. Hartley, P.B. Mitchell. Front row: Miss Duerdon, Miss Patchett, Mr Thoringer, Mrs T. Wilkinson, Mrs J. Asman, Mrs G. Garstang. (Courtesy of Clitheroe Museum)

Edisford Bridge, 1960s. In 1339 two landlords repaired a bridge damaged by floods. It was originally one of the fording places on the River Ribble, and the site of a thirteenth-century hospital for lepers dedicated to St Nicholas. 'No lepers at Edsford for some years past' was recorded in 1350.

A revolutionary way to advertise, 1908: 'Firth and Son, Ideal Bakery, Clitheroe, offer fresh cakes daily.' James H. Firth of Duck Street was noted for his oat cakes and Lancashire parkin. The primitive aeroplane was superimposed on the old photograph.

The Clitheroe Orpheus Glee Singers, with their then fashionable gold guards, moustaches and white 'dickies', sang at concerts in and around the town at the turn of the century. Commencing as handbell ringers, on 4 May 1898 they began glee singing, conducted by George Waddington.

Castle Street, 1920. By this time motor cars and motor cycles with side cars had made an appearance. On the right is the White Lion Inn. The 'big lamp', now gone, is being used as a signpost to Sabden.

Councillor J. Thornber. Councillor Thornber was Mayor of Clitheroe twice, from 1919 to 1920 and from 1920 to 1921. He was the great-grandfather of the four Thornber brothers who presently run Holmes Mill in Greenacre Street. There were originally three buildings on this site: a foundry established by James Alston, and a size house and spinning mill erected in 1823 by John Taylor. The Mercer family built the New Mill in 1830, and also acquired the foundry and added a weaving shed. Eventually 700 looms and 16,000 spindles were being operated, but dwindling trade led to part of the buildings being used as Clitheroe Technical School in 1916. Following renovation, James Thornber of Burnley took over in 1906. James's grandfather had been a hand-loom weaver at Rimington.

Lizzie Taylor, one of Luke Taylor's daughters, in a photograph taken by Mr Broughton of Clitheroe, *c.* 1890. Her sisters were Martha, Mary Alice, Ann, Esther, Edith, Emma, Sarah and Laura; her brothers were Tom, Jack, Henry, Luke and Charlie. Lizzie had a daughter of her own named Laura.

Another daughter of Luke Taylor, possibly Esther, photographed in 1890 by Clitheroe photographer Mr Forrest, who lived opposite the Town Hall in Church Street.

Clitheroe Castle, from St James's Church, *c.* 1930. Revd George Fielden, a former rector of St James's, 1852–93, disliked floral decorations in church, declaring, 'The House of God is not the place to hold a horticultural show.'

The River Ribble, *c.* 1930. A sharp curve about ¼ mile from Brungerley was known as 'Dangerous Corner'. On one occasion when the river, whose source is on Cam Fell, was in flood the Grindleton ferry boat capsized here as it was coming to Brungerley Farm. The men were rescued by quarry workers and the boat, worth £1, by Eli Tucker.

Four Pendle Valley mill girls show a spirit of comradeship early this century. The 1892 Slater's Directory lists seventeen cotton spinners and manufacturers in Clitheroe. John Brooks in Factory Lane and William Braithwaite of Henthorn Mill were cotton waste dealers.

Clitheroe Ladies' Morris Team, 1920. The team was formed in 1919 and disbanded in 1937. It is seen here under the direction of Mr Winkley. The original men's team, formed in 1884, danced the North-West Morris style until 1913. This style was revived by the team of ladies.

Peace Day celebrations, Low Moor, 1945. A children's party was one of the special events.

Holmes Mill, the premises of James Thornber Ltd, 1956. This picture was presented by the employees to mark the firm's Golden Jubilee, from 1906 to 1956, a time when sateens, fents, twills and shirtings were made. Today, novelty fabrics using man-made fibres are produced.

Browsholme Hall, *c.* 1900. For centuries this was the ancestral home of the Parkers (see p. 11), who were Bowbearers of Bowland Forest. The hall was rebuilt in 1604 and improved in the 1800s. Ancient manuscripts, the 'doggange' and a heavy silver seal giving Puritan ministers the right to preach were kept at this hall near Clitheroe.

King Street, Clitheroe, May 1911. On this postcard the post office is indicated with a cross. In the coaching days of the 1850s mail was collected from the premises of Baileys, Corn Millers of York Street.

Four Clitheroe 'tacklers' at Salford Bridge Mills at the time of King George V's coronation, 1911. Among the decorations is a portrait of Queen Mary. These mills, second only to Low Moor Mills, reached their zenith in 1883.

The proclamation of Edward VII as King was read out in Market Place in 1901, obviously on a very wet day.

Railway Road, *c.* 1900. In Railway Yard Newton Aspden, Arthur Clapham, Robert Dugdale and Brooks & Pickup of Burnley were all coal merchants, during a time when the mills and railway needed plentiful supplies.

Mr J. Garnett, on horseback, with the Clitheroe deputation that visited the Waterworks, 1905. Annual inspection was made by the Mayor, councillors and officials. The manager at the office in Church Street was Joseph Barrett, whose home was in Lower Gate near that of William Bennett, bill poster and bellman.

Outside the White Lion amidst medals, bunting and best clothes for Coronation Day, 1911. In the middle is Mayor Clement Taylor Mitchell riding in a landau with Clitheroe council officials.

Mr Sainsbury, clothier and outfitter, 1909. The shop displays a full range of garments to combat the winter weather in Clitheroe, including flat, cloth caps which men wore both outdoors and in the mills. No fewer than seventeen milliners were available for ladies.

An all-male group outside Mr Heaton's Railway View Inn 'licensed to sell ale, porter and tobacco'. The bizarre effigy was used in a Clitheroe torchlight procession which celebrated the end of the First World War in August 1919. Another torchlight procession was held in 1948, assembling in Chatburn Road and proceeding via York Street, Castle Street, Parson Lane, Bawdlands, Edisford Road, Henthorn Road, Eshton Terrace, Greenacre Street, Whalley Road, Moor Lane, Wilkin Street and Hayhurst Street to Shaw Bridge where the procession dispersed. Two hours later, at 10.30 p.m., there was a fireworks display from the castle keep which, along with the Grammar School, was floodlit. However, neither procession could outclass the 'monster' torchlight procession which had been held in 1897. In its attempt to celebrate Queen Victoria's Diamond Jubilee, Clitheroe Bicycle Club provided 'a feast of lanterns' headed by 'the world-renowned Clitheroe Borough Prize Band'. The Clitheroe steam fire-engine burned coloured fire along the route. Sir John Finch in his state chariot was attended by his 'cork drawer, chief bottle washer, ale tasters and other high civic officials'.

The Clitheroe General Post Office 'indoor and outdoor staff', 1930s. Note the telegram delivery boy at the front. Directories of the time show that mail collections and deliveries occurred frequently throughout the day.

The four Liberal Party candidates in Clitheroe, early 1900s. Left to right: Mr Aitken, Mr Westhead, Mr Miller and Mr Jackson. Mr Thompson of Primrose Mill was a leading Liberal in the early 1900s.

Roby House, Clitheroe, *c.* 1910. In 1890 this was the home of a wealthy Manchester stockbroker, Thomas Duckworth Benson, the Socialist editor of the magazine *Uses*. His son George was educated at Clitheroe Grammar School and later became a Member of Parliament. At Roby House Mr Duckworth Benson entertained the leading Socialists of the day: Scottish Socialist leader Ramsay Macdonald, James Keir Hardie, Tom Mann and Harry Quelch. This gathering is probably one such occasion. Many of his guests 'spoke from the big lamp in Clitheroe Market Square and caused a sensation' according to the *Clitheroe Advertiser and Times*, who also dubbed T.D., as he was known, 'a live wire' who managed to influence politically his doctor, 'none other than Dr Alfred Musson, an ultra-Tory'. Frequent visits to Roby House led Philip Snowden to speak at Blackburn Market Ground and be selected as Blackburn's parliamentary candidate. The house is now known as Barraclough House.

The large work force outside one of the bobbin shops in Clitheroe, 1885. This gives some indication of the numbers employed in the various mills, including Mitchell's in Moore Lane, Christopher Cowgill's Waterloo Saw Mills, the paper manufacturers, Carlisle & Son of Primrose Mills and many others.

A 10 ton road roller owned by the Eddison Steam Roller Company crashed in Church Brow on 12 September 1930, effectively closing the road at a point opposite Prospect House. One side of the steering gear had broken.

Episode 11 in the Clitheroe Pageant, presented on 31 July and 7 August 1948 to mark the 800th anniversary of the granting of Clitheroe's first Charter of Freedom. Twenty episodes gave a pictorial representation of scenes from Clitheroe's history from 1148 to 1948. Local headmasters Arthur Langshaw and Lawrence Hardy, along with H.B. Shaw, organist and choirmaster of Clitheroe Parish Church, wrote the pageant, which was staged in the castle grounds. Reserved seats cost 3s 6d. Episodes included Paulinus and the conversion of Ribblesdale, the foundation of Clitheroe Parish Church, the Pilgrimage of Grace, the trial of the Lancashire Witches, Thomas Jollie and the Puritans of Ribblesdale, and a highwayman on Clitheroe's main road.

Locomotive 42558 in Clitheroe station, 1960s. The engine is heading a train eagerly awaited by a group of people who look ready to start out on their summer holiday.

The water wheel at Primrose Mill, *c.* 1910. Founded by James Thompson, the mill was equipped with looms and 1,000 spindles and earned a national reputation for calico printing, but when King Cotton slumped many workers left for America, and the huge mill became premises for three different firms.

Castle Gate, *c.* 1900. This is one of the oldest parts of Clitheroe, at the top of Castle Street, with the signpost to Whalley. Until piped water arrived in 1855, three wells were the main sources of water for this area, first and foremost being St Mary's Well in Well Terrace.

The smartly turned-out fire brigade at Chatburn Road End, 1905. TD 6730 is the registration number of their fire-engine. In earlier years the brigade would have had to use a manual engine, fitted with an exhausting hand-pump and requiring two horses to pull it.

Parson Brow with the Castle Inn on the left, *c.* 1925. In 1885 William Hardacre was listed as a Refreshment Room Keeper at 1 Parson Lane, lower down. The lane was so named because Revd Thomas Wilson of the Grammar School used to live there.

Railway Avenue, with the strong stone walls typical of Clitheroe, *c.* 1918. Built in 1851, parallel with the railway, the avenue linked King Street and Waddington Road. In the 1880s Jackson and Bleazard, contractors dealing in all kinds of building materials, had premises at Railway View.

James L. Bulcock and Son of Regent House at the junction of Railway Road and King Street, 1909. The outfitters were offering Dexter macintoshes and rainproof overcoats for the winter season. They were the registered agents for famed Burberry garments.

Moor Lane Congregational Chapel, July 1911. Members are arriving for Professor H. Duff's Sunday address. This chapel dates from 1852, although a Congregational Chapel was opened in Wellgate in 1815.

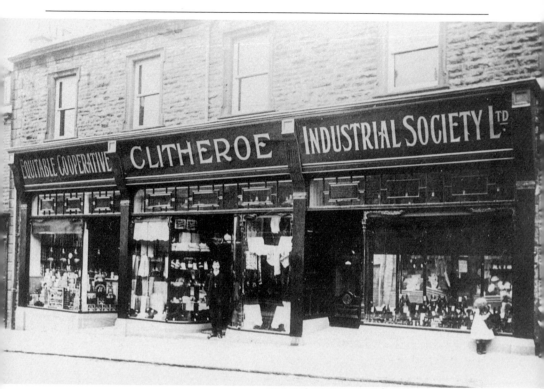

Moor Lane Clitheroe Equitable Co-operative Industrial Society Ltd, *c.* 1890. The prices of the goods piled in the shop windows were revealed in the Clitheroe *Advertiser and Times*: Scotch whisky *2s 9d* a bottle; bacon *7d* a pound; beer *1s 6d* per gallon. Christmas Clubs were run to ease the burden of payment, customers putting aside *6d* a week in the months approaching the festive season. Members of one club were offered: 'Christmas cake, raspberry sandwich, biscuits, macaroons, ½lb mincemeat, lemon cheese, 6 mince pies and one of the prettiest pictures that has ever been published entitled Life's Springtime' – all for *5s.*

The Singer Sewing Machine shop,
50 Lower Gate, Salford, *c.* 1892. James
parker was the sewing machine agent.
The Whalley New Road through
Salford was opened in 1809.

A great day at Jack Hall's fish shop,
c. 1920. The poster announces the
'wonder of the world, the most
handsome fish in British Waters,
Lampris Luna', which was caught off
Scotland by Pete Brown and delivered
by Oscar Cleve and Son for sale in
Clitheroe. Mr Hall, wearing straw
boater, was also well known for poultry
and game. The River Ribble long
offered some of the finest stretches for
trout and salmon fishing. There is a
record at Clitheroe Museum that 'the
hatching of the first trout and first
salmon in the Southern Hemisphere
took place here on the 4th and 5th May
1864'.

Clitheroe town from the castle, 1960s. The intensity of the town's growth is evident. The two chimneys of Portland Cement can be seen on the left. Housing, business premises and traffic have increased but the centuries-old structure is still discernible. The old town was close confined between castle and church, the castle being quickly perceived as an excellent defensive position. Sixty settlers were encouraged to form a community by being offered plots or burgages but without onerous duties to the lord. By the seventeenth century there were about 600 people living in the old town of thatched roofs, with the Grammar School and the Moot Hall adding to the main buildings. In May 1979 a fire at the parish church caused £300,000 worth of damage. Restoration took place and the organ was rebuilt by George Sixsmith. Double glazing the clerestory windows was part of the programme.

War Memorial, Clitheroe, 1970. In 1920 the castle and its 16½ acres of grounds passed to the people of Clitheroe, purchased by the Borough Council from Lord Montagu. All wished it to become a memorial to those who had died in the First World War. The money was raised very enthusiastically and in many ways by the men, women and children of Clitheroe and a total of £15,000 was realized, which also paid for essential work to the grounds. The Garden of Remembrance was formed later and included a memorial to Clitheroe men who died in the Boer War. On special celebrations the bronze soldier figure at the Cenotaph and the castle keep are floodlit.

A cutting through the snow has been made on Worston Road. The exceptional snowfall in 1940 covered the fells and blocked roads. Schools were closed, cars abandoned, but lorry ETB 769 was determined to get through.

A military procession passes Clitheroe Library during the Second World War. People responded generously when their patriotism was appealed to, as the crowds watching this procession demonstrate. War Weapons Week was held on 8–14 March 1941.

Clitheroe's main street with Clitheroe Library (centre) and Church Street (left), 1971. To cope with the increased traffic and pedestrians, road markings and a crossing with Belisha beacons have been introduced.

Two workmen look out from James Thornber Ltd, 1956. Improvements have been made to Holmes Mill in Greenacre Street, notably the re-roofing of sheds.

The Bowling Green, part of the castle grounds, 1970. In 1948 children's sports were held on the castle playing fields, including pony riding and jumping, with refreshments provided. Former residents living abroad who wished to share in the Borough's celebration sent money to buy sweets for the children, which were distributed at the castle bandstand. A grand concert was given by 'The Tonics', which included the Winterton duo, Angela and Helen, two girls in harmony, and operatic baritone Frank Lord. Sheepdog demonstrations and an old folks' party were all part of the fun.

Playing fields and children's recreation area below the keep of Clitheroe Castle, 1970. On the occasion of the 800th Charter Celebrations, at 6.30 p.m. on Saturday 7 August 1948 musical rides and spectacular events by the Mounted Branch of the Lancashire Constabulary were staged, by kind permission of the Chief Constable of Lancashire, Captain Sir Archibald F. Horden. The castle keep was floodlit and a fireworks display was held at 10.30 p.m.

A team from Nelson and Colne College of Further Education, 1976. The volunteers put together a 'talking newspaper', *Pendle Voice,* for the blind people of Pendle. Hours after the papers appeared, tape-recorded condensed versions of the news were delivered to the blind and partially sighted. From left to right: Violet Ashton, Douglas Barber and Glynis Harrison, who were well assisted by Carole Thursby and Betty Bennett (not shown). (Courtesy of *Lancashire Life*)

Town Crier Roland Hailwood and clog maker Bill Turton, 1980s. Thwaites' Heritage Campaign involved a line up of town criers at Clitheroe and a range of crafts including bodging, thatching, clogging and wheelwrighting. Displays were held in other parts of Lancashire including Barrowford and Nelson. Although there are no outstanding public buildings in Clitheroe, it has a store of enviable traditions arising from its long history.

Wellsprings Inn near Clitheroe, *c.* 1940. Not far from here is a heap of stones known as the Devil's Apronful. The story goes that when the Devil threw a huge stone at Clitheroe keep he burst his apron strings with the effort and out rolled all the boulders. The Devil did manage to make a large hole in the keep, visible to this day.

Three Clitheroe children mischievously peep through the metal railing of the ancient keep, 1960s. The castle keep, a gatehouse and surrounding ditches with defensive walls were all built by the Normans from limestone quarried nearby.

WHALLEY, SAWLEY AND PENDLE HILL

Downham village with Pendle Hill, 1904.

The Lancashire and Yorkshire Railway station at Clitheroe, 1900s. The station was busy on summer bank holidays when visitors poured in to visit Brungerley for the boating. They also filled up horse-drawn wagonettes which conveyed them to Whalley Abbey, Downham, Gisburn, Slaidburn, Pendle Hill and other villages for tours of the Ribble and Hodder valleys. Carey's Restaurant in King Street and The Café, Market Place, where Taylor and Hughes were proprietors, supplied 'noted pork pies, morning coffee and afternoon tea'. Read's Tearooms at Grindleton catered for large parties and the Hodder Vale Café on the main road from Mytton to Whitewell was famed for its 'unequalled views of the beautiful valley and glorious sunsets'. Most of the wagonettes were supplied by J.R. Garlick's stables in Wellgate. Pack-horse routes starting from Clitheroe had developed into such roads as those over Whalley Nab and Nick o' Pendle. At one time 1,000 pack horses a day passed Causeway House, the last Lime Gal (pony) dying in 1902.

The ruins of Whalley Abbey, 1960. Part of the layout and the north-east gateway are shown. Founded in 1296, this great Cistercian abbey had five stages of building, the first stone being laid on St Barnabas Day, 12 June. Adam de Huddleton gave a quarry in the fourteenth century which ushered in a busy period of construction. The building of the church was begun by Abbot Robert when two more quarries became available to use. Abbot Paslew, the last abbot, added the Lady Chapel between 1521 and 1536 and he also rebuilt the Abbot's Lodging and the north-east gateway. It was reported in the seventeenth century that 'Sir Robert Assheton pulled down the old steeple and the walls adjoining the cloister walls next to the dovecote and the great window at the head of the stairs in the cloister.' Sir Ralph was known 'to regale his tenants with beef, bread and good brown ale'.

The north-east gateway at Whalley Abbey, *c*. 1903. At the Dissolution of the Monasteries under Henry VIII's decree much stone vanished but the Abbot's Lodging remained intact, becoming the residence of the Assheton family in 1536. In the early 1880s the abbey mill was destroyed. It is obvious that the original group of twenty monks from Stanlaw who moved to Whalley and commenced building under Abbot Gregory de Northbury quickly acquired an amount of property in the neighbourhood of Whalley.

Whalley Church, from the ruins of the abbey, 1960. The abbey church was dismantled by Sir Ralph Assheton and the stone used for his own purposes, improving his dwelling, after the death of Abbot Paslew who was hanged, drawn and quartered. A Whalley printer bought the remains of Whalley Abbey in 1836 and the ruins were later restored in the Gothic style much favoured in those days.

Whalley Abbey ruins, 1907. Original tiles have been revealed in the Chapter House where monks assembled daily to hear a chapter from the rule of St Benedict. Here, any monk who had misbehaved was flogged, but abbey accounts show that the brothers lived well, spending £40 annually on wine, and enjoying imported luxuries such as figs, raisins, dates, ginger and currants.

King Street, Whalley, c. 1900. Mrs Day's confectioner's shop is on the left and a heavy farm cart lies idle. The Georgian houses remain today. The Whalley Arms, now the Hog's Head, dates from the eighteenth century. The Swan was the chief coaching inn on the route to Manchester.

The Abbot's Lodgings, Whalley Abbey, 1921. Today, weekend courses are held in the manor-house, which once belonged to the Asshetons but is now owned by Blackburn Diocese. Of the ground plan of the great church where the monks prayed eight times a day, the altar has been restored and is used for open-air communion.

Pollard's Fancy Depository (left) and, higher up, the Whalley Arms, 1900. Sett-paved King Street is busy with horse-drawn delivery carts. On the right is the De Lacy Arms Inn. The Saxon village of Whalley was possibly built on a Roman site to connect with the fort at Ribchester.

The spectacular Whalley viaduct, built in the 1840s and bridging the valley and River Calder, has forty-nine arches and is over 2,000 ft long. Special trains and a regular service delight visitors now that the line has been reopened.

Broad Lane, Whalley, c. 1913. Clay from the railway embankment was used to make the viaduct arches. Thirteen brickmakers placed the bricks in wagons and after firing, these were drawn up in wheelbarrows pulled by horses.

Sawley Abbey, 1900. By 1904 the ruins of the abbey were covered with ivy and undergrowth. Founded in 1147, this was a daughter house of Fountains Abbey but the monks had a hard time raising crops on an often waterlogged site. Salley or Sawley means damp or willow-grown.

The impressive arches, which can be seen when approaching Sawley Abbey, photographed here in 1890. One of the arches had to be removed many years later as it obstructed the highway. It now makes an imposing entrance to a farm field. The screen in the Mitton Church of All Hallows came from Sawley Abbey.

Church Street, Colne, from Sutcliffe's Corner, 1890. At the trial of the Lancashire Witches the story emerged that pedlar John Law of Colne was asked for pins by Mother Demdike's granddaughter Alizan. When he refused to give her any she immediately cursed him and he suffered a stroke. He recovered sufficiently to testify at the trial.

Worston Hall, *c.* 1908. The hall is also connected with the so-called Witches of Pendle, and was part of the Honour of Clitheroe, as was Chatburn. In the thirteenth century John de Lacy demanded, as well as his rents, two dog collars and a pair of gloves payable on the feast of St Oswald.

Pendle Hill rising above Downham village shown on a Lancashire and Yorkshire Railway series postcard, 1905. This was the country area used in Harrison Ainsworth's novel *The Lancashire Witches*. In 1964 Pendle Hill was included in a 300 square mile region which was designated an area of outstanding natural beauty.

Pendle Hill and the reservoir, 1921. The hill, 7 miles long and 1,831 ft high, shelters Clitheroe from the east. The reservoir solved the problem of flash floods which from time to time had plagued the villages. No one in his right senses ever took the path through Pendle Forest at night.

Picturesque Downham village, 1961. The village had been so well safeguarded by succeeding squires that at this time it looked little different from 100 years previously. Each cottage had a stone slab in front which crossed the duck-laden brook that runs through the village. Since 1653 the children of Downham were educated at the village school. The present building was provided by William Assheton in 1839, but in 1985 it closed as a day school. Described as the prettiest village in the shadow of Pendle, it was the reputed haunt of the Lancashire Witches whose fame or infamy continues to arouse intense interest. It was also known for 'Downham diamonds', large quartz crystals found in the local limestone. Sir Ralph Assheton paid 5s for a particularly large one in the seventeenth century.

Roughlee with Pendle in the background, 1941. Roughlee was once associated with hand-loom weaving but is better known because of Alice Nutter, who lived at Roughlee Hall. Silent throughout her trial as a witch, she was condemned in 1612 and hanged with the others.

Whitewell Hotel and the Hodder Valley, 1901. This area offers another view of Pendle, where superstition prevailed for centuries ('Oft on Pendle's side one hears a passing sound of distant bells . . .'). In 1842 local man Samuel Bamford called Pendle Hill 'a leviathan reposing amid billows'.

Section Three

SURROUNDING

VILLAGES

*Stonyhurst College, Cromwell's Bridge and
'Paradise', 1904.*

Peace Day at Bashall Eaves, September 1919. One of twelve Saxon battles fought by King Arthur is supposed to have been by Bashall Brook. The lords of Bashall Hall went down in history for their treachery towards King Henry VI, although they were well rewarded. The king was seized at the hypping (stepping) stones, Brungerley.

Repairing the White Bear Inn, Barrowford, 1912. This ancient building was made for the Hargreaves family in 1607. It was close to the Toll House in turnpike days. Bear baiting gave the inn its name.

Bolton-by-Bowland's Market Cross near the Coach and Horses Inn, 1960s. The village has two greens. The ancient Forests of Bowland, Pendle, Gisburn and Rossendale appointed ale tasters among their officials. The last of these was Richard Taylor or 'Spindle Dick'. He had kept a beer house with an inn sign showing a globe with the head and shoulders of a man protruding, bearing the legend 'Help me through the world'. Above his beer shop Taylor taught a Bible class every Sunday and for his ale-tasting he made a pewter gill measure fitted with an ebony handle in the shape of a cross. Each October he attended the Halmot Court in Haslingden to be reinstated. After the ceremony a meal was provided for all the officers of the forests.

BOLTON-BY-BOWLAND MOTOR SERVICE

A

Frequent and Reliable Service between

LOW MOOR, CLITHEROE,
CHATBURN, WORSTON.
SAWLEY
and BOLTON-BY-BOWLAND
TIME TABLES ON APPLICATION.

Proprietor - - I. BLEAZARD

Copy Nook Garage,
BOLTON-BY-BOWLAND.

Bolton-by-Bowland Motor Service, whose proprietor was I. Bleazard, operated from Copy Nook Garage in 1930 to Low Moor, Clitheroe, Chatburn, Worston and Sawley. Eventually the service was run by the Ribble Bus Company. Bolton-by-Bowland might have developed as a spa village as, like other parts of Pendle, it has a mineral spring near Fooden Hall whose waters, smelling of sulphur, were said to increase fertility. In the Church of St Peter and St Paul is a memorial to Sir Ralph Pudsay who died in the fifteenth century. He had three wives and twenty-five children.

The skeleton of the horse 'Balloon Boy' with those of an unknown man and a dog early this century. These were kept in the harness room at Bolton Hall until the contents of the hall were auctioned in the 1950s prior to demolition. It is thought that the macabre collection went to Stonyhurst College after the sale. Bolton Hall, home of the Pudsay family, was where Henry VI hid for a while after his defeat at the Battle of Hexham, only to be captured later at Brungerley. William Pudsay made a spectacular leap on horseback from Rainsber Scar across the river to make good his escape after being charged with counterfeiting silver shillings, the silver ore coming from mines on his own estate near Rimington.

A group outside Hacking Hall, Billington, c. 1900. Hacking Hall is a seventeenth-century manor-house situated on the left bank of the River Calder close to where it joins the Ribble. The house, with its mullioned windows and stone-slated roofs, was built by Sir Thomas Walmesley in 1607. The original oak door studded with heavy iron nails is still in existence but fireplaces have been altered and oak wainscots removed. Other richly carved oak panelling bearing Judge Walmesley's initials was removed and taken to Dunkenhalgh in 1874.

Chatburn Mill Fire, 10 October 1905. This cotton mill had been converted from a corn mill in 1823. More successful was Victoria Mill, which Robert Hargreaves and William Ingham established in 1858 from a silk hand-loom workshop.

Chatburn Mill Christmas Party, *c.* 1923. Twenty-three happy ladies from Beamer's Preparation Department are enjoying the occasion. Besides cotton manufacturing limestone was quarried at Chatburn. Bold Venture, opened in 1836, was extended when the Bolton and West Yorkshire Railway built a special siding to cope with the transporting of lime.

A Chatburn Whitsuntide procession passing the Black Bull Inn, 1930s. My grandfather recalled the quack doctor of Chatburn who sold 'universal pills', one only to each customer and never to a doctor for fear of analysis. This quack doctor, aged 80, was swept to his death one winter trying to ford the river.

Heys Farm Adult School Guest House, West Bradford, shown in a photograph taken by the Clitheroe photographer E. Buck, early 1900s. This is an early example of such a guest house. The village, whose name means broad ford, is a mile from Horrocksford Bridge.

The Traveller's Rest, formerly the New Inn, 1906. This idyllic country scene at Dale Head was lost forever when Stocks Reservoir near Slaidburn was filled. The post office and the blacksmith's shop, both busy in 1900, also disappeared.

Chapel House Farm, Dale Head, 1913. This building was also destroyed when Stocks Reservoir was created.

Sheep Clipping, Lamb's Hill Farm, Dale Head, around the turn of the century. The drought of 1911 caused great water shortages in the crowded holiday resort of Blackpool and as a result the Fylde Water Board Act of 1912 authorized the taking of head water from the River Hodder. Two and a half thousand acres of land were acquired and the building of Stocks Reservoir commenced in 1920. To service this a temporary village for hundreds of navvies was set up at Hollins. Dale Head disappeared when the reservoir was filled. The foundations of the Traveller's Rest, a favourite calling place for motorists, farms like Lamb's Hill and other buildings have reappeared at low water during dry summers.

Downham village, 1960. A custom over 250 years old was still being observed in the 1930s when the Assheton sermon was preached by Revd J.A. Latham, the vicar of Read. Held annually on 30 January, the sermon was referred to as 'the Downham preaching'. Although there was a different vicar every year, the remuneration, £12, never varied. A similar custom was preserved at Whalley on 5 February where the clergyman also received £12. The dates of the sermons originated in the will of Sir Ralph Assheton of Whalley in 1680. In each case the preacher was confined to one of two texts: Job, chapter 19, verses 25–7 or Colossians, chapter 3, verses 3–4.

Downham Old Hall, 1924. Downham Old Hall is a picturesque, two-storey building with low, mullioned windows and a porch. The abbeys of both Whalley and Sawley had land in Downham.

Another view of Downham village, c. 1910. Cottagers kept hens and grew fruit and vegetables. In the 1880s a cottager would receive one shillingsworth of provisions for thirty eggs taken to a Clitheroe shopkeeper. 'Blue' or skimmed milk was priced at 30 quarts for 1s.

This newspaper photograph, captioned 'the new squire, the late squire (seated) and the heir to the estates', refers to the Asshetons of Downham in 1904. Since the days of Nicholas Assheton, who kept an interesting journal in the seventeenth century, the family have controlled the village from Downham Hall. Originally a Tudor mansion, it was greatly altered in 1834. Stone cottages were built at Chapel Brow for weavers in the eighteenth century and the village has remained unspoiled. Road making during that century revealed the remains of two Roman soldiers. A Roman road ran north of the village and workmen also found an urn containing a large hoard of coins, 1,000 silver denarii, which were taken to Downham Hall. The Pudsays of Bolton and the Listers of Gisburn were two other prominent Ribblesdale families.

Downham, 1925. The Church of St Leonard can be seen on the left facing the Assheton Arms. John Paslew, the last Abbot of Whalley, who was executed in 1537 for the influence he had on the Pilgrimage of Grace, presented an octagonal font to the church. It was said that 100 years ago the Parson of Downham kept a football in the pulpit and after service he kicked off at the church gates, using the length of the village street as a football pitch. The ducks of Downham, at home on the stream that runs through the village, attract today's visitors.

Low Moor post office, early 1900s. The post office was obviously somewhere to gather and gossip, especially if the street photographer was busy with his camera recording shops, houses and villagers. On the left is a horse-mounting block. This seventeenth-century building was close to the entrance of Low Moor Cotton Mill which adjoined the village. Houses were built for the operatives of this huge factory, one of the first water-powered spinning mills in Lancashire. In the 1780s it was called Edisford Factory, being north of Edisford Bridge. The venture was partially financed by the Clitheroe banker and lawyer John Parker, later joined by Jeremiah Garnett, who came to Low Moor from Yorkshire in 1799. As the mill became larger, power-loom weaving was introduced: '32,000 spindles and 2,500 pieces of cotton goods weekly' was recorded by James Baines in his 1828 Lancashire Directory.

Lower Hodder Bridges, May 1917. Here on 10 June 1138 the Scots defeated the English at the Battle of Clitheroe. Oliver Cromwell's army passed through Clitheroe twice and a council of war was held here in 1648. It has been said of this 'paradise' area: 'Three rivers with perfect fishing and too many bridges to count.'

The blacksmith's forge at Waddington, 1900. Smithy Cottage is next door and the village stocks were also in this vicinity.

Waddington Hospital residents outside the chapel with the chaplain, *c.* 1890. The name of the hospital may be derived from an Anglo-Saxon chieftain, Wada, who is said to have camped at Waddington before the Battle of Langho.

Waddington Road, 1890. The road here reveals a very different aspect from that of today, with its antique lamp, old weavers' cottages of stone, slate, many chimneys and sixteen-paned windows with glazing bars, few of which now survive.

The Waddington Peace Victory Celebration, 1919. This photograph presents a study in the fashions of the day. Grandmothers, mothers and daughters with babies in perambulators all join in happily.

The Waddington Choir outside the Wesleyan Chapel prepare to set off in a wagonette on a choir outing, 1901. Next to the top-hatted driver is Mr R. Southworth, smoking a pipe.

The Brass Room at the Moor Cock Inn, Waddington, when Walter Greenwood was proprietor, c. 1920. The Moor Cock, or 'Ye Moor Cock Inn' as it was advertised, had a nine-hole golf-course and putting green in the hotel grounds. In the 1880s when my father visited with my grandfather, 'duck and green peas' was the standing dish at this well-known inn and people came from miles around to sample it. Grandfather Edward Hoghton married Catherine Garnett of Low Moor and they eventually moved to Belthorn. Their children were Jonathan, William Edward, Louise, Clement (see p. 34) and Arthur.

Burnley Road, Gisburn, 1920. Gisburn was once a busy market town noted for its cattle sales. Stagecoaches rattled through en route to Yorkshire. Landowner Thomas Lister built the Ribblesdale Arms, which had extensive stabling facilities for the large numbers of horses needed in the days of the Turnpike Trusts.

Gisburne Park Gates, 1906. A famous herd of white cattle grazing the parkland until the 1850s were said to be bred from the herd kept at Whalley Abbey. When the monastery was dissolved the beasts were lured by sweet music from their pastures to Gisburne Park.

Gisburn's main street, 1906. On the right beyond the cottages is the Ribblesdale Arms. The last Lord Ribblesdale who lived at Gisburne Park died in 1925 and the title became extinct.

Grindleton, 1906. The village is known for Roger Brearley, founder of a radical religious sect not unlike the Quakers. He was curate at Grindleton Church from 1615 to 1622 and much persecuted. The village had a felt hat works when 'chimney pot' hats were popular.

Crow Wood, Hurst Green, *c.* 1900. There was a bobbin mill here in the eighteenth century. As early as 1826 the road from Hodder Bridge to Hurst Green was constructed under the direction of J.L. Macadam, using his revolutionary tarmacadam process.

The Shireburne Almshouses, 1962. Originally these were built 3 miles away at Kemple End in 1706, but in 1946 they were dismantled and reassembled at Hurst Green for use by workers at Stonyhurst College.

Waddow Hall, near Clitheroe, *c*. 1927. By this time the hall had been bought by the Girl Guides Association. At one time it belonged to the Garnett family, cotton manufacturers of Low Moor, and is said to have a ghost, Peg O'Nell, who every seven years demands a death by drowning in the Ribble.

West Bradford, 1920. The village dates back to the reign of Edward II. Here during the Industrial Revolution a corn mill was turned into a cotton mill, a process which happened in other Pendle villages. The corn mill at Gisburn became a saw mill in 1911.

This beer shop, photographed in 1902, was typical of many throughout towns and villages around Clitheroe, with its fine lamp and display boards: 'Draught beer and stout drawn from the wood. Fine sparkling ales.' Such premises also sold provisions – sugar, salt, oatmeal, treacle and so on – for which customers brought their own containers. On certain nights such delicacies as fruit and meat pies and parched peas were available; shop hours were very long, some shops staying open until midnight.

An initial stone at Pendleton, 1914. The initials, I.I.T. 1693, refer to Thomas Jollie, stonemasons rendering J as I in those days, and the initial of the family name coming first. Ejected from his living, Jollie wandered the countryside preaching non-conformity. In the late seventeenth century he had a licensed meeting-place, Wymondhouses, where he finally built a chapel that became a centre for non-conformists from miles around. Well into the nineteenth century a memorial service was preached for Thomas Jollie in the ruins of Wymondhouses, the last remains of which vanished in 1890.

Mitton village, 1906. All Hallows Church, built in Edward III's reign, contains the splendid Shireburne Chapel and a leper squint. The two hamlets of Little Mitton and Great Mitton, separated by the River Ribble, were once in Lancashire and Yorkshire respectively.

The ferry boat at Hacking End, crossing the River Ribble near Mytton, 1898. (In later years the spelling became Mitton.) So old that nobody knows when it started, the penny crossing was discontinued in the 1930s.

Morris dancers, brass bands and Britannia beneath a large Union Jack in a Colne Whitsuntide procession, *c.* 1920. The famous hymn tune Rimington, composed by Francis Duckworth from a Pendle village of that name, was sung for the first time in Colne in 1904. At Pendleton twenty-two massed choirs performed it: 'Jesus shall reign where'er the sun.'

The eighteenth-century post office, Pendleton, 1890. The tiny postmistress is Ellen Haworth. The oldest building in this unspoilt village mentioned in the Domesday Book is Spring House Farm. A branch of the Hoghton family settled at Pendleton.

Stonyhurst Gate House, *c.* 1920. For 400 years, until the line died out, the Shireburn family lived at Stonyhurst where each generation made changes. The great building with towers and cupolas was part of the design under Sir Nicholas Shireburne in the eighteenth century but tragedy struck the family when the son and heir died after eating yew berries. In 1717 on Nicholas's death the estate passed to his daughter who had married the Duke of Norfolk. In 1794 Thomas Weld, a descendant, leased Stonyhurst to a Jesuit teaching order who had lost their own school and it became the famous Roman Catholic public school, attended by such well-known figures as poet Gerard Manley Hopkins and actor Charles Laughton. It was the first public building to be lit by gas, in 1811.

Stonyhurst Observatory, *c.* 1912. The Jesuit owners of Stonyhurst College organized a repair and reconstruction programme to suit their specific needs, building St Peter's Church between 1832 and 1835. Classrooms, dormitories, observatory, museum and library were added or reorganized. The Refectory is part of the Elizabethan house of Sir Richard Shireburne whose family provided the village school in Hurst Green and the almshouses near Ribchester. Sir Richard lived at Stonyhurst for almost sixty years and was a Master Forester of Bowland and Steward of the Manor of Slaidburn.

Slaidburn, near Clitheroe, *c*. 1900. Situated on the right bank of the River Hodder near Dunnow Hill, the village was virtually isolated until the introduction of the Bounty Bus Service in the 1930s. At that time a curfew bell was still rung each night.

Slaidburn Brass Band, *c*. 1900. Long established, the Brass Band commenced as a Silver Band. Clitheroe Borough Brass Band under Bandmaster Joseph Douglas won seven prizes in seven contests in 1884. A Fife and Drum Catholic Band was formed in Clitheroe in 1859.

George Robinson, clogger and shoe repairer. George had his shop at Catlow Farm, Slaidburn, around the 1920s. Nicholas Assheton's diary refers to: 'Fishing with nets at Slaidburn. Gott some 47 fishes and later gott 65 fish above Newton.'

Mr Turner of Slaidburn (centre) with the clog soles which he used to cut out by hand and stack for drying, c. 1909. The soles were fashioned from lengths of wood and finished on foot-operated buffing machines fitted with emery wheels and leather-covered wheels for polishing. Clog irons and leather uppers were then fitted.

The bridge spanning the River Hodder at Slaidburn, photographed in 1960, has always been a pleasant spot for a picnic. Another fine bridge spans Croasdale Beck, a tributary of the Hodder The name of the inn, Hark to Bounty (previously the Dog Inn), commemorates the fox hound Bounty, one among a favourite pack which hunted from Slaidburn. In an upper room of the inn, oak benches and the dock from days when it was a forest court can still be seen. St Andrew's, 'the Church at Slaydeburn', was referred to in the twelfth century during the reign of Henry I when Hugh de Laval granted interest in it to the monks of Kirkby Priory. Its strongly built church tower gave protection to both people and cattle when raids from Scotland were feared.

Sheep washing at Buckmire Farm, *c.* 1890. The farm was situated at the confluence of the River Hodder and Croasdale Beck, Slaidburn. Mr William Carr is in the sheep pen. Slaidburn means 'washing of sheep', which has been done there for centuries.

Chatburn Welfare Society having a 'knife and fork' tea at Victoria Mill, 1939. On 30 October 1940 German bombs extensively damaged shops and killed several villagers including Miss Alice Robinson, a Chatburn benefactress.

DUNSOP BRIDGE TO
RIBCHESTER

Higher Whitewell Farm, c. 1909.

The old stables at Thorneyholme, Dunsop Bridge, *c.* 1960. Here the Towneley family, who built nearby St Hubert's Church in 1865, bred racehorses, notably Kettledrum.

Whitewell Hotel from the bridge, *c.* 1921. On the side of the inn there used to be a lodge which served as a courtroom, Whitewell being the administrative centre of Bowland. St Michael's Church, rebuilt in 1836 and served from Chipping, contains a fine Flemish tapestry from Browsholme Hall.

Sykes Farm, the Trough of Bowland, 1923. At Sykes lime burning took place to enrich the farmland, and during the early nineteenth century many trees were planted on Mr Fenton Cawthorne's 1,500 acres in the Trough.

Worston, early 1900s. Crow Cottage in the village had a circular window, reputedly designed for a witch to fly through on her broomstick. A relic from bull-baiting days is a strong, iron ring in the ground where the bull was tethered and taunted by dogs to tenderize the flesh, prior to slaughter.

Edmund Parkinson outside the School House in Bowland, 1920. At his home at Higher Core, as a boy, Edmund remembered seeing the leather jerkin tough enough to deflect weapons, worn by his ancestors. Edmund married Mary Hoyle of Chipping, a schoolmistress. Landowner James Garnett presented £1,000 for building the school.

Berry Lane, Longridge, *c.* 1901. The lane may derive its name from the benefactor James Berry of Alston whose charity was established in 1803. He gave £200 to Seth Eccles, a tanner, son of Thomas, a cotton spinner. The annual interest from this was to be distributed among the poor and distressed.

The boundary stone at the head of the Trough of Bowland, 1964. Situated 1,000 ft above sea-level, the stone denoted the limits of the counties of Lancashire and Yorkshire. Clitheroe and Whitewell were then in Yorkshire but this changed in 1974. The stone is still there overlooking the same wild and primeval landscape, unchanged in centuries apart from the disappearance of trees from the higher slopes of the fells. The Lancashire Witches passed this spot on their way to Lancaster Castle where they were tried and hanged on 20 August 1612 following cross-examination by Roger Nowell at Read Hall.

Mr Richard Place and Mrs Mary Place. Mr and Mrs Place farmed at Greenside in Bowland in the 1890s in one of the vaccaries said to have originated as land given to twelve soldiers who had fought valiantly for the king. The laying out of upland pastures from the vaccaries of the Forest began in the fifteenth century. Royal Forest policy was to develop Wyresdale and Bleasdale as great vaccary systems of beef and dairy farms. The ancient forest of Bleasdale covered 7,298 acres and extended to the boundary stone between Lancashire and Yorkshire at Sykes.

The post office at Wray, 1904. This village is interesting as far as Clitheroe history is concerned because Captain Cuthbert Bradkirk came from there. Left in charge of Clitheroe Castle, he repaired the damage done by Prince Rupert's attack and increased its defences, but after the Royalist army was defeated at Marston Moor he and his men left in a hurry, knowing that Cromwell's army was passing through the Ribble Valley. At that time the population of Clitheroe was about seven hundred. Another of Clitheroe's famous names is Captain James King FRS, the son of James King, vicar of Clitheroe from 1743 to 1773. Educated at Clitheroe Grammar School, he sailed with Captain Cook on his world voyage.

The view from Harling, Chipping, photographed by E. Buck of Clitheroe, 1902. Towards the skyline can be seen St Bartholomew's Church, famed for its ancient yew tree from which the bows of the Chipping White Jackets were made. Innkeeper Thomas Bleasdale was buried beneath the yew on 16 August 1767.

The Jacksons, a Quaker family, farmed here at Ortner on the edge of Bowland Forest in the 1890s. John Bright, who attended the Quaker School at Newton-in-Bowland in 1826, said he learned there 'to fish, to take wasps' nests and to eat oatcake'.

Saddle End Farm, Chipping, on 'a perfect day, March 30th 1929'. Between Clitheroe and Whalley, apart from such farms as Waller House, Moor Farm, Elmridge, Kirkcroft and Daub Hall, the only hostelry for miles was the Bailey Hey inn, which by the 1930s had also become a farm.

Brabbins School, Windy Street, Chipping, c. 1919. The 1684 datestone bears the initials of John Brabbin, as well as those of local men Christopher and Robert Parkinson, John Hawthornthwaite and Richard Marsden. John Brabbin was a local cloth maker who left money to endow this village school.

PUBLIC NOTICE.

At a Meeting of the **Master Cloggers** of Tyldesley, Hindsford and District, it was unanimously agreed that on and after OCTOBER 27th, 1913, the following

LIST OF PRICES

should be CHARGED FOR CLOGS, in consequence of the advance in Wages, Material, Etc.

NEW CLOGS.			RE-CLOGGING.		
MEN'S.					
Size	Best New	Second New	Size		
13	5 1	4 6	13		
13	5 0	4 5	13	1 8	
11	4 10	4 3	11		
10	4 8	4 0	9		
WOMEN'S.			**WOMEN'S**		
8	4 2	3 8	8		
7	4 0	3 4	7	1 6	
6	3 8	3 3	6		
4	3 4	2 10	5	1 4	
3	3 2	2 8	3		
2	3 0	2 6	2	1 3	
1	2 10	2 4	1		
13	2 8	2 4	13		
11	2 6	2 4	11	1 2	
10	2 4	2 2	10		
8	2 2	2 0	8		
7	2 0	1 10	7	1 1	
5	1 11	1 8	6		
5	1 10	1 8			
4	1 10	1 8			

RE-IRONING	3½d. per Set
SHANKS IRONS	4½d. per Set

All BOOTS CLOGGED charged 2d. per pair more than the above List.
All CAPPELS on Customers Clogs charged 1d. each, if more than two.
All CLOGS RE-CLOGGED with extra Brass Nails, 1d. per pair more.

Signed on behalf of the Masters

JAMES KERSHAW, Chairman.
JOHN HAUGHTON, Secretary.

This list of prices, dated 27 October 1913, was agreed by master cloggers and prevailed over a wide area. In Clitheroe alone there were ten cloggers in 1900. The top price for new clogs was only 5s and for re-clogging between 1s 1d and 1s 8d, according to size. Fresh clog irons were 3½d a set. W.J. Garnett of Bleasdale Tower built a reformatory in Bowland where thirty young lawbreakers were disciplined. Among other crafts they were instructed in clogging and one returned to become Bleasdale's clogger. Fancy clogs were worn for clog-dancing.

Blacksmiths, early 1930s. Because of the continuing demand for horses to be shoed and farm implements to be made and repaired this was another busy trade. The post office at Bleasdale was once a smithy with a glowing forge to cope with horse riders and pack-horse trains which passed its door. On the slopes of Fairsnape can be seen sledge rows, scrapes on the fell sides indicating the route taken by loads of peat cut from Bowland's moors for delivery to farms and the blacksmith's forge.

The White Bull Hotel, Ribchester, 1902. The licensee at the time was William Haigh. Water Street on the Roman road north begins from this old coaching inn. The long-gowned lady stands beside a horse-mounting block from the eighteenth century. The pillars supporting the porch are thought to be of Roman origin, taken from a temple in use for 300 years when the Romans had a fort at Ribchester, an important station with a constant influx of legions from other forts. In 80 AD the Roman general Agricola decided to build this fort close to the ford over the River Ribble, where the triple-arched bridge now stands.

'Chariots Only', a humorous reference by Military Police in 1961 to Ribchester's days as a Roman fort. *Bremetennacum Veterandrum* was the Roman name for Ribchester. A cavalry group of 500 men and horses was stationed here and there is record of a rector Droghu and his horse being drowned when attempting to ford the River Ribble. The 6 acres of the fort included a bath house, granary and temple. Excavation went on in 1913. The recently refurbished museum houses Roman artefacts including a copy of the best find of all, made on the river bank in the late eighteenth century along with twenty-four other artefacts: a bronze ceremonial parade helmet which is now in the British Museum.

A carving which survived from Hothersall Hall and which serves as a reminder that the Lords of the Manor of Ribchester once owned the ancient hall. Thomas Tyldesley's diary for 10 June 1714 refers to 'young Mr Hothersall'. In 1882 Jonathan Openshaw, born 7 May 1805, a native of Bury, lived at Hothersall. A hard-working woollen manufacturer, he gave generously to the poor and became one of the foremost landed proprietors in the district. He pulled down the historic residence and improved the land. In recognition of his kindness to the poor a drinking fountain was provided in his memory and a tablet placed in Ribchester Church.

HERE LYETH INTOM: TWO WYVES OF ROBERT PARKINSON OF FAYRESNAPE GENT: VIZ:

MARIE DAVGHTER OF IEROM ASHETON GENT:(DISCENDED OF THE HOVSE OF MIDLETON WHERE SHE WAS BORNE) HE HAD ISSVE BY HER, MARIE, ROBTE, ELIZABETH, & THE 4TH LYETH WITH HER HERE, MARY & ROBTE LYE IN HEIGHSAM CHVRCHE WHERE THEIRE FATHER IS PATRON: SHE WAS MARYED 4OR YEARES, 7NE MONETHES AND 5: DAYES AND DYED THE 7TH OF APRILL AO DÑI 1615:/

ANNE DAVGHTER OF GEORG: SINGLETON OF STAYNINGE ESQVIER, HE HAD ISSVE BY HER MARIE, GRACE, ANNE RAPHE, AND GEORGE, SHE WAS MARYED 7NE YEARES AND TEN DAYES AND DYEI THE XXITH OF NOVEMBER AO DÑI 1623:/

THEIRE PTES THEIRE PSONS & THEIRE VERTVOVS LYFE, NOW REST IN PEACE FREED FROM THE BONDE OF WYFE.

The Parkinson Memorial brass in Chipping Church, which details the virtuous lives of Robert Parkinson's two wives in the early seventeenth century. Of this large family with representatives in many parts of Lancashire, William Parkinson of Chestnut Row, Downham, was the oldest inhabitant, aged 90 in 1921. He owned the only wireless set, with earphones, tuned to Station 2ZY. Son of a hand-loom weaver, he had lived in Downham for fifty years. He played the cello and was choir master at Chatburn Church. For their cottage industry the Parkinsons had two pairs of hand looms which, in order for the family to make a living, had to be kept going. Warps and wefts were obtained from Roughlee to where the finished cloth was returned – a long walk for William with heavy bolts of cloth to carry. He had also served as a pedlar, hawking goods around the villages as far as Bolton-by-Bowland. He recalled that when he was a small boy, if someone had an accident and broke a bone, the patient was galloped on horseback to the 'bone-setter' in Haslingden.

Chaigley Hall Manor was used as a Red Cross Hospital *c.* 1916. A priest, caught administering the Roman Catholic Mass when it was forbidden to do so, was beheaded at Chapel House Farm. His head was tossed into a field but Mrs Holden of Crawshaw gathered it in her apron and also rescued the missal, altar cloth and candles. There were then kept secretly at Chaigley.

The parish church of St Lawrence, Longridge, 1920. The church was built as a chapel of ease because of the great distance to walk to St Wilfrid's, Ribchester. It was rebuilt in 1716 and the tower added in 1822. This was a poor, ecclesiastical district until endowed with land in Goosnargh.

Outside St Wilfrid's Church, Ribchester, 1964. So much adding and rebuilding over the centuries resulted in a reference to the church as 'an irregular pile' in a nineteenth-century engraving. A musicians' gallery or 'singing pew' for performers on bassoon, fiddle and serpent was installed in 1736. Announcements would be made from the steps leading up to the old sundial.

Stydd Almshouses, Ribchester, 1965. These were built by John Shireburn of Stonyhurst in 1726, and were intended for 'five old and infirm women faithfully professing the Catholic faith'.

The foundations of part of the Roman granaries, Ribchester, 1965. In the fourth century the Roman garrison left the fort, after which it must have fallen into ruin. Excavations began as early as 1883. The granaries came to light in 1889 and later the bath house. Revd J. Shortt traced the fort wall; John Garstang uncovered the west gate of the fort and many sections of the surrounding walls in 1914. That year, in which the museum opened amidst great public interest, also saw the discovery of the Commanding Officer's house. The many hand mills or stone querns that have been found indicate that much grain was grown in the district. In the 1960s Ribchester Museum was a National Trust property administered by a small local committee.

St William's, Lee House, Thornley, *c.* 1920. Thomas Eccles of Thornley, who was registered as a 'papist' in 1717, founded this Roman Catholic church in 1758. The postcard was issued by Alfred Lewty of the Post Office.

Stydd Church, near Ribchester, *c.* 1924. In 1886 an outdoor service was held at 'the venerable church which claims to be 700 years old and at which tradition affirms the Apostle Paul preached'. As it was the only building that remained standing during a severe earth tremor, the origin of its name is said to be 'Stood'.

Longridge Church Choir outing to Clitheroe, 1917. Members are standing outside the Longridge Industrial Co-operative Society grocer's shop. Shrove Tuesday was considered the greatest neighbour-seeing day of the year in Longridge and Goosnargh. Housewives 'made a peculiar kind of pancake' and children ranged from house to house begging toffee and gingerbread. Clothing Clubs, established in 1841 (subscription 4d a week), enabled new clothes to be bought at Whitsuntide. In the 1840s Alice Becketh was the most famous old woman in the Longridge area 'for gingerbread and fairy tales'. Another character was Laithwaite Oates, a 'wild, wandering, homeless being famous for idiotical fun, mischief and almost unearthly ugliness'. At a 'lating of the witches' on Longridge Fell in the nineteenth century Laithwaite played a trick causing all the candles held by the group to go out simultaneously. (The Year's Notes, 1870)

'We are having a busy time', is the message on the front of this postcard, sent in August 1908. 'I have had my likeness taken with my other tent mates', continues the message on the back, from the Longridge Detachment, 4th Battalion, B Company.

Tom Hawthornthwaite, who became miller at Thornton, *c.* 1906. Seen here in the Longridge lanes, Tom rode all over the Fylde and beyond Bowland. Cycling was so popular that Mr Ashton of Thornton post office had a penny-farthing bike which he took to the Isle of Man.

A men's outing from the Corporation Arms, Longridge, *c.* 1919. One of Mercer's charabancs is being driven by Mr Thistleton.

Queen's Mill, Longridge, 1951. Built in 1875, the mill produced curtaining, sateens and cambrics. When weaving ended here in 1964 the Longridge Manufacturing Company Ltd went into voluntary liquidation. The plant was auctioned and the sale included 200 silk and cotton looms.

Acknowledgements

I would especially like to thank Mrs Laura Clark for her generous help and shared interest, also the many people of Clitheroe and round about who greeted me warmly and gave freely of their time in my search for information and photographs.

C. Ainsworth • Stanley Butterworth • *Clitheroe Advertiser and Times*
Clitheroe Library • Clitheroe Museum • Clitheroe Tourist Office
Vicki Greenwood • Derek Hawthornthwaite • J.D. Hodgkinson
Susan Holden • Michael Jackson • David Joy • W.L. King • Lancashire Library
Lancashire Life • Lancashire Record Office • Vivian Meath • Mary Parker
Red Rose Postcard Club • *Ribble Valley Explorer* • Mike Rothwell
Ron Severs • Ian Spencer • Mark Thornber • Stephen Thornber
Hans Van Dike • Whalley Library • Mr H. Wilkinson • Mary Wynn

BRITAIN IN OLD PHOTOGRAPHS

To order any of these titles please telephone 01903 721596

ALDERNEY

Alderney: A Second Selection, *B Bonnard*

BEDFORDSHIRE

Bedfordshire at Work, *N Lutt*

BERKSHIRE

Maidenhead, *M Hayles & D Hedges*
Around Maidenhead, *M Hayles & B Hedges*
Reading, *P Southerton*
Reading: A Second Selection, *P Southerton*
Sandhurst and Crowthorne, *K Dancy*
Around Slough, *J Hunter & K Hunter*
Around Thatcham, *P Allen*
Around Windsor, *B Hedges*

BUCKINGHAMSHIRE

Buckingham and District, *R Cook*
High Wycombe, *R Goodearl*
Around Stony Stratford, *A Lambert*

CHESHIRE

Cheshire Railways, *M Hitches*
Chester, *S Nichols*

CLWYD

Clwyd Railways, *M Hitches*

CLYDESDALE

Clydesdale, *Lesmahagow Parish Historical Association*

CORNWALL

Cornish Coast, *T Bowden*
Falmouth, *P Gilson*
Lower Fal, *P Gilson*
Around Padstow, *M McCarthy*
Around Penzance, *J Holmes*
Penzance and Newlyn, *J Holmes*
Around Truro, *A Lyne*
Upper Fal, *P Gilson*

CUMBERLAND

Cockermouth and District, *J Bernard Bradbury*
Keswick and the Central Lakes, *J Marsh*
Around Penrith, *F Boyd*
Around Whitehaven, *H Fancy*

DERBYSHIRE

Derby, *D Buxton*
Around Matlock, *D Barton*

DEVON

Colyton and Seaton, *T Gosling*
Dawlish and Teignmouth, *G Gosling*
Devon Aerodromes, *K Saunders*
Exeter, *P Thomas*
Exmouth and Budleigh Salterton, *T Gosling*
From Haldon to Mid-Dartmoor, *T Hall*
Honiton and the Otter Valley, *J Yallop*
Around Kingsbridge, *K Tanner*
Around Seaton and Sidmouth, *T Gosling*
Seaton, Axminster and Lyme Regis, *T Gosling*

DORSET

Around Blandford Forum, *B Cox*
Bournemouth, *M Colman*
Bridport and the Bride Valley, *J Burrell & S Humphries*
Dorchester, *T Gosling*
Around Gillingham, *P Crocker*

DURHAM

Darlington, *G Flynn*
Darlington: A Second Selection, *G Flynn*
Durham People, *M Richardson*
Houghton-le-Spring and Hetton-le-Hole, *K Richardson*
Houghton-le-Spring and Hetton-le-Hole:
    A Second Selection, *K Richardson*
Sunderland, *S Miller & B Bell*
Teesdale, *D Coggins*
Teesdale: A Second Selection, *P Raine*
Weardale, *J Crosby*
Weardale: A Second Selection, *J Crosby*

DYFED

Aberystwyth and North Ceredigion,
    Dyfed Cultural Services Dept
Haverfordwest, *Dyfed Cultural Services Dept*
Upper Tywi Valley, *Dyfed Cultural Services Dept*

ESSEX

Around Grays, *B Evans*

GLOUCESTERSHIRE

Along the Avon from Stratford to Tewkesbury, *J Jeremiah*
Cheltenham: A Second Selection, *R Whiting*
Cheltenham at War, *P Gill*
Cirencester, *J Welsford*
Around Cirencester, *E Cuss & P Griffiths*
Forest, The, *D Mullin*
Gloucester, *J Voyce*
Around Gloucester, *A Sutton*
Gloucester: From the Walwin Collection, *J Voyce*
North Cotswolds, *D Viner*
Severn Vale, *A Sutton*
Stonehouse to Painswick, *A Sutton*
Stroud and the Five Valleys, *S Gardiner & L Padin*
Stroud and the Five Valleys: A Second Selection,
    S Gardiner & L Padin
Stroud's Golden Valley, *S Gardiner & L Padin*
Stroudwater and Thames & Severn Canals,
    E Cuss & S Gardiner
Stroudwater and Thames & Severn Canals: A Second
    Selection, *E Cuss & S Gardiner*
Tewkesbury and the Vale of Gloucester, *C Hilton*
Thornbury to Berkeley, *J Hudson*
Uley, Dursley and Cam, *A Sutton*
Wotton-under-Edge to Chipping Sodbury, *A Sutton*

GWYNEDD

Anglesey, *M Hitches*
Gwynedd Railways, *M Hitches*
Around Llandudno, *M Hitches*
Vale of Conwy, *M Hitches*

HAMPSHIRE

Gosport, *J Sadden*
Portsmouth, *P Rogers & D Francis*

HEREFORDSHIRE

Herefordshire, *A Sandford*

HERTFORDSHIRE

Barnet, *I Norrie*
Hitchin, *A Fleck*
St Albans, *S Mullins*
Stevenage, *M Appleton*

ISLE OF MAN

The Tourist Trophy, *B Snelling*

ISLE OF WIGHT

Newport, *D Parr*
Around Ryde, *D Parr*

JERSEY

Jersey: A Third Selection, *R Lemprière*

KENT

Bexley, *M Scott*
Broadstairs and St Peter's, *J Whyman*
Bromley, Keston and Hayes, *M Scott*
Canterbury: A Second Selection, *D Butler*
Chatham and Gillingham, *P MacDougall*
Chatham Dockyard, *P MacDougall*
Deal, *J Broady*
Early Broadstairs and St Peter's, *B Wootton*
East Kent at War, *D Collyer*
Eltham, *J Kennett*
Folkestone: A Second Selection, *A Taylor & E Rooney*
Goudhurst to Tenterden, *A Guilmant*
Gravesend, *R Hiscock*
Around Gravesham, *R Hiscock & D Grierson*
Herne Bay, *J Hawkins*
Lympne Airport, *D Collyer*
Maidstone, *I Hales*
Margate, *R Clements*
RAF Hawkinge, *R Humphreys*
RAF Manston, *RAF Manston History Club*
RAF Manston: A Second Selection,
    RAF Manston History Club
Ramsgate and Thanet Life, *D Perkins*
Romney Marsh, *E Carpenter*
Sandwich, *C Wanostrocht*
Around Tonbridge, *C Bell*
Tunbridge Wells, *M Rowlands & I Beavis*
Tunbridge Wells: A Second Selection,
    M Rowlands & I Beavis
Around Whitstable, *C Court*
Wingham, Adisham and Littlebourne, *M Crane*

LANCASHIRE

Around Barrow-in-Furness, *J Garbutt & J Marsh*
Blackpool, *C Rothwell*
Bury, *J Hudson*
Chorley and District, *J Smith*
Fleetwood, *C Rothwell*
Heywood, *J Hudson*
Around Kirkham, *C Rothwell*
Lancashire North of the Sands, *J Garbutt & J Marsh*
Around Lancaster, *S Ashworth*
Lytham St Anne's, *C Rothwell*
North Fylde, *C Rothwell*
Radcliffe, *J Hudson*
Rossendale, *B Moore & N Dunnachie*

LEICESTERSHIRE

Around Ashby-de-la-Zouch, *K Hillier*
Charnwood Forest, *I Keil, W Humphrey & D Wix*
Leicester, *D Burton*
Leicester: A Second Selection, *D Burton*
Melton Mowbray, *T Hickman*
Around Melton Mowbray, *T Hickman*
River Soar, *D Wix, P Shacklock & I Keil*
Rutland, *T Clough*
Vale of Belvoir, *T Hickman*
Around the Welland Valley, *S Mastoris*

LINCOLNSHIRE

Grimsby, *J Tierney*
Around Grimsby, *J Tierney*
Grimsby Docks, *J Tierney*
Lincoln, *D Cuppleditch*

Scunthorpe, *D Taylor*
Skegness, *W Kime*
Around Skegness, *W Kime*

LONDON

Balham and Tooting, *P Loobey*
Crystal Palace, Penge & Anerley, *M Scott*
Greenwich and Woolwich, *K Clark*
Hackney: A Second Selection, *D Mander*
Lewisham and Deptford, *J Coulter*
Lewisham and Deptford: A Second Selection, *J Coulter*
Streatham, *P Loobey*
Around Whetstone and North Finchley, *J Heathfield*
Woolwich, *B Evans*

MONMOUTHSHIRE

Chepstow and the River Wye, *A Rainsbury*
Monmouth and the River Wye, *Monmouth Museum*

NORFOLK

Great Yarmouth, *M Teun*
Norwich, *M Colman*
Wymondham and Attleborough, *P Yaxley*

NORTHAMPTONSHIRE

Around Stony Stratford, *A Lambert*

NOTTINGHAMSHIRE

Arnold and Bestwood, *M Spick*
Arnold and Bestwood: A Second Selection, *M Spick*
Changing Face of Nottingham, *G Oldfield*
Mansfield, *Old Mansfield Society*
Around Newark, *T Warner*
Nottingham: 1944–1974, *D Whitworth*
Sherwood Forest, *D Ottewell*
Victorian Nottingham, *M Payne*

OXFORDSHIRE

Around Abingdon, *P Horn*
Banburyshire, *M Barnett & S Gosling*
Burford, *A Jewell*
Around Didcot and the Hagbournes, *B Lingham*
Garsington, *M Gunther*
Around Henley-on-Thames, *S Ellis*
Oxford: The University, *J Rhodes*
Thame to Watlington, *N Hood*
Around Wallingford, *D Beasley*
Witney, *T Worley*
Around Witney, *C Mitchell*
Witney District, *T Worley*
Around Woodstock, *J Bond*

POWYS

Brecon, *Brecknock Museum*
Welshpool, *E Bredsdorff*

SHROPSHIRE

Shrewsbury, *D Trumper*
Whitchurch to Market Drayton, *M Morris*

SOMERSET

Bath, *J Hudson*
Bridgwater and the River Parrett, *R Fitzhugh*
Bristol, *D Moorcroft & N Campbell-Sharp*
Changing Face of Keynsham,
  B Lowe & M Whitehead

Chard and Ilminster, *G Gosling & F Huddy*
Crewkerne and the Ham Stone Villages,
  G Gosling & F Huddy
Around Keynsham and Saltford, *B Lowe & T Brown*
Midsomer Norton and Radstock, *C Howell*
Somerton, Ilchester and Langport, *G Gosling & F Huddy*
Taunton, *N Chipchase*
Around Taunton, *N Chipchase*
Wells, *C Howell*
Weston-Super-Mare, *S Poole*
Around Weston-Super-Mare, *S Poole*
West Somerset Villages, *K Houghton & L Thomas*

STAFFORDSHIRE

Aldridge, *J Farrow*
Bilston, *E Rees*
Black Country Transport: Aviation, *A Brew*
Around Burton upon Trent, *G Sowerby & R Farman*
Bushbury, *A Chatwin, M Mills & E Rees*
Around Cannock, *M Mills & S Belcher*
Around Leek, *R Poole*
Lichfield, *H Clayton & K Simmons*
Around Pattingham and Wombourne, *M Griffiths,*
  P Leigh & M Mills
Around Rugeley, *T Randall & J Anslow*
Smethwick, *J Maddison*
Stafford, *J Anslow & T Randall*
Around Stafford, *J Anslow & T Randall*
Stoke-on-Trent, *I Lawley*
Around Tamworth, *R Sulima*
Around Tettenhall and Codsall, *M Mills*
Tipton, Wednesbury and Darlaston, *R Pearson*
Walsall, *D Gilbert & M Lewis*
Wednesbury, *I Bott*
West Bromwich, *R Pearson*

SUFFOLK

Ipswich: A Second Selection, *D Kindred*
Around Ipswich, *D Kindred*
Around Mildenhall, *C Dring*
Southwold to Aldeburgh, *H Phelps*
Around Woodbridge, *H Phelps*

SURREY

Cheam and Belmont, *P Berry*
Croydon, *S Bligh*
Dorking and District, *K Harding*
Around Dorking, *A Jackson*
Around Epsom, *P Berry*
Farnham: A Second Selection, *J Parratt*
Around Haslemere and Hindhead, *T Winter & G Collyer*
Richmond, *Richmond Local History Society*
Sutton, *P Berry*

SUSSEX

Arundel and the Arun Valley, *J Godfrey*
Bishopstone and Seaford, *P Pople & P Berry*
Brighton and Hove, *J Middleton*
Brighton and Hove: A Second Selection, *J Middleton*
Around Crawley, *M Goldsmith*
Hastings, *P Haines*
Hastings: A Second Selection, *P Haines*
Around Haywards Heath, *J Middleton*
Around Heathfield, *A Gillet & B Russell*
Around Heathfield: A Second Selection,
  A Gillet & B Russell
High Weald, *B Harwood*
High Weald: A Second Selection, *B Harwood*
Horsham and District, *T Wales*

Lewes, *J Middleton*
RAF Tangmere, *A Saunders*
Around Rye, *A Dickinson*
Around Worthing, *S White*

WARWICKSHIRE

Along the Avon from Stratford to Tewkesbury, *J Jeremiah*
Bedworth, *J Burton*
Coventry, *D McGrory*
Around Coventry, *D McGrory*
Nuneaton, *S Clews & S Vaughan*
Around Royal Leamington Spa, *J Cameron*
Around Royal Leamington Spa: A Second Selection,
  J Cameron
Around Warwick, *R Booth*

WESTMORLAND

Eden Valley, *J Marsh*
Kendal, *M & P Duff*
South Westmorland Villages, *J Marsh*
Westmorland Lakes, *J Marsh*

WILTSHIRE

Around Amesbury, *P Daniels*
Chippenham and Lacock, *A Wilson & M Wilson*
Around Corsham and Box, *A Wilson & M Wilson*
Around Devizes, *D Buxton*
Around Highworth, *G Tanner*
Around Highworth and Faringdon, *G Tanner*
Around Malmesbury, *A Wilson*
Marlborough: A Second Selection, *P Colman*
Around Melksham,
  Melksham and District Historical Association
Nadder Valley, *R. Sawyer*
Salisbury, *P Saunders*
Salisbury: A Second Selection, *P Daniels*
Salisbury: A Third Selection, *P Daniels*
Around Salisbury, *P Daniels*
Swindon: A Third Selection, *The Swindon Society*
Swindon: A Fourth Selection, *The Swindon Society*
Trowbridge, *M Marshman*
Around Wilton, *P Daniels*
Around Wootton Bassett, Cricklade and Purton, *T Sharp*

WORCESTERSHIRE

Evesham to Bredon, *F Archer*
Around Malvern, *K Smith*
Around Pershore, *M Dowty*
Redditch and the Needle District, *R Saunders*
Redditch: A Second Selection, *R Saunders*
Around Tenbury Wells, *D Green*
Worcester, *M Dowty*
Around Worcester, *R Jones*
Worcester in a Day, *M Dowty*
Worcestershire at Work, *R Jones*

YORKSHIRE

Huddersfield: A Second Selection, *H Wheeler*
Huddersfield: A Third Selection, *H Wheeler*
Leeds Road and Rail, *R Vickers*
Pontefract, *R van Riel*
Scarborough, *D Coggins*
Scarborough's War Years, *R Percy*
Skipton and the Dales, *Friends of the Craven Museum*
Around Skipton-in-Craven, *Friends of the Craven Museum*
Yorkshire Wolds, *I & M Sumner*